GREAT QUOTES FOR CAREGIVERS

*Words to help inspire and sustain
the caregiving journey*

Compiled and edited
by Craig Hlas

For Jill

I care tons.//Craig

COPYRIGHT

© 2019 by Craig Hlas.

Contact the editor: cjhlas@outlook.com

Cover by Alex Albornoz.

Published by Postcards From The Wedge, LLC
P.O. Box 2101
Cedar Rapids, Iowa
52406-2101

If you find "Great Quotes For Caregivers" interesting or helpful, I would be very grateful if you would consider leaving a review with a few kind words."

CONTENTS

PREFACE

The term "caregiver" might sound simple, but the reality is complex.

Each caregiver is one of hundreds of millions with a common experience, but each one's experience differs from all others. The shared bond centers on serving the immediate and long-term needs of people who are sick, injured, recovering, failing, falling, and rising.

Your life as a caregiver can disrupt any or all other aspects of life, and you might sometimes feel isolated or in need of support and inspiration in different ways.

The expectations you have for yourself as a caregiver — and the unfamiliar and numerous tasks you must undertake and skills you must acquire immediately or over time — can sometimes be overwhelming. And of course, caregiving is not something done in isolation of your other roles and responsibilities.

◆ ◆ ◆

Yet caregiving can yield astonishing personal growth and satisfaction.

Overcoming disappointments and setbacks, working through tough moments or months, and discovering you actually *got this* (or that) — it's all food and fuel for the caregiver. The rewards manifest themselves in remarkable ways.

◆ ◆ ◆

My wife Jill suffered a stroke in 2013. As a result, I became a caregiver — or as I sometimes say, an "enhanced personal assistant."

We've gone through many ups and downs since then, almost continuously facing new challenges. Before, I knew no next to nothing about strokes — let alone how to care for someone else so intensively at times. (Not counting my time as a parent some years ago.)

I also know the subtle joy of achieving seemingly small breakthroughs along the way.

I've learned to work more patiently to become more patient over the past few years. And I've strived to become a better cook, laundry folder, housekeeper, appointment driver, gardener, bath helper, hangnail-clipping assistant, and whatever else comes my way from one moment to the next.

Caregivers realize they're a work in progress.

There's plenty of trial and error learning involved on the climb to a higher caregiving plateau.

Ultimately, you learn because you have to. You accept any support or supportive ideas that come your way. And in my case, knowing that so many caregivers do much more than I do, often in far more forbidding circumstances, humbles me daily.

Sometimes caregivers just need to refresh their emotional sensibilities or overcome physical weariness. They need to reclaim their sense of mission and motivation. That's where this book comes in.

As curator and editor, I've discovered potent and inspiring thoughts can come from authors, philosophers and teachers, actors and comedians, athletes, and (to no one's surprise) caregivers themselves.

*"I always love to quote Albert Einstein because no-
body dares contradict him."*
—Studs Terkel

This book started as a personal collection of quotes that made me more keenly aware of the type of caregiver I wanted and needed to become. It grew from that into a more detailed, organized compilation of qualities and characteristics I think most caregivers are likely to aspire to (or in some cases, hope to subdue).

You'll find hundreds of quotations here — with a few from Einstein — in more than 50 categories.

◆ ◆ ◆

"I hate quotations. Tell me what you know."
—Ralph Waldo Emerson

You do know a lot, but it doesn't hurt to tap into other people's observations about life. The eminently quotable Emerson and so many others cited in this book have much to say about resilience, overcoming, gathering your hope, reinforcing your energy, staying positive, confronting setbacks and suffering, and creating an atmosphere of enthusiasm and optimism. The variety of pieces make a tapestry almost as complex as caregiving itself.

As a caregiver, your focus is on doing good without any expectation of tangible rewards. Yet the richness of your actions — and interactions — makes you a hero, whether you would consider yourself one or not.

Even heroes need a break sometimes, though. Caregivers can give only so much without needing to recharge and restore a sense of calm, tranquility, and inner peace. Selflessness does not mean neglecting yourself, and sacrifice does not mean giving until you're used up.

The quotations like in this book can be hard-hitting or subtle, serious or ironic. Many of them cross two or more categories, but I tried to put them where they seemed to fit best.

◆ ◆ ◆

"One original thought is worth a thousand mindless quotings."
— Diogenes

Original thoughts can spring from the thoughtful musings of others — something said in a speech, written in an essay, or planted in the voice of a fictional character.

These quotes are mindless only in that they cannot by themselves do what caregiving ultimately requires: consistent, loving action. But they can help you shift an attitude or motivate you in a way that fosters a greater sense of satisfaction and success as a caregiver.

I hope you're challenged, inspired, and given some solace by "Great Quotes For Caregivers."

"Listen to me now
I need to let you know
You don't have to go it alone."
— U2

◆ ◆ ◆

— Craig Hlas

CAREGIVING: STEP BRAVELY

You may be just one person, but to one person you may be the world.

— Brandi Snyder

One person caring about another represents life's greatest value.

—Jim Rohn

The closest thing to being cared for is to care for someone else.

— Carson McCullers, *The Square Root of Wonderful*

Caregiving is universal. There are only four kinds of people in the world — Those who have been caregivers, those who currently are caregivers, those who will be caregivers, and those who will need caregivers.

— Rosalynn Carter

There is no exercise better for the heart than reaching down and lifting people up.

—John Andrew Holmes Jr.

Offering care means being a companion, not a superior. It doesn't matter whether the person we are caring for is experiencing cancer, the flu, dementia, or grief.

— Judy Cornish

Caregiving often calls us to lean into love we didn't know possible.

— Peggi Speers and Tia Walker, *The Inspired Caregiver*

Sometimes our work as caregivers is not for the faint of heart. But, you will never know what you are made of until you step into the fire. Step bravely.

— Deborah A. Beasley

Caregiving has no second agendas or hidden motives. The care is given from love for the joy of giving without expectation, no strings attached.

> — Gary Zukav

Caregiving will never be one-size-fits-all.

> — Nancy L. Kriseman

Family caregivers can go a long way toward helping parents or other loved ones stay in their own homes, but only if they understand the challenges of caregiving and know how to get help and support.

> — Denise Logeland, *10 Things Every Family Should Know*

Being thrust into the role of caregiver without any preparation is difficult under any circumstances.

> — Carol Levine

I believe that most caregivers find that they inherit a situation where they just kind of move into caregiving. It's not a conscious decision for most caregivers, and they are ultimately left with the responsibility of working while still trying to be the caregiver, the provider, and the nurturer."

> — Sharon Law Tucker

If you're someone people count on, particularly in difficult moments, that's a sign of a life lived honorably.

> — Rachel Maddow

Affirmations are our mental vitamins, providing the supplementary positive thoughts we need to balance the barrage of negative events and thoughts we experience daily.

> — Peggi Speers and Tia Walker, *The Inspired Caregiver*

Caregiving has us managing two lives and balancing both.

> — Unknown

Many of us follow the commandment 'Love One Another.' When it relates to caregiving, we must love one another with boundaries. We must acknowledge that we are included in the 'Love One Another.

> — Peggi Speers and Tia Walker, *The Inspired Caregiver*

When you're a caregiver, you need to realize that you've got to take care of yourself, because, not only are you going to have to rise to the occasion and help someone else, but you have to model for the next generation.

> —Naomi Judd

To care for others I need to take care of me.

> —Unknown

It is so important as a caregiver not to become so enmeshed in the role that you lose yourself. It's neither good for you nor your loved one.

> —Dana Reeve

Care work produces public goods, and should be supported in families by policies such as paid parental leave and caregiver tax credits, and by investments in good training and wages for caregiving, including early childhood education, in the market.

> —Riane Eisler

Caregivers, both paid and unpaid, hold together the fabric of our society and should be honored, supported, and recognized.

> —Wendy Lustbater

Anxiety happens when you think you have to figure out everything all at once. Breathe. You're strong. You got this. Take it day by day.

> —Karen Salmansohn

CHANGE: FACING IT, MAKING IT

The straight line cannot proceed through the torturous twists of life.

—Giambattista Vico

To find perfect composure in the midst of change is to find Nirvana.

—Shunryu Suzuki

When the winds of change blow, some build walls and others build windmills.

—Chinese proverb

Change comes like a little wind that ruffles the curtains at dawn, and it comes like the stealthy perfume of wildflowers hidden in the grass.

—John Steinbeck

All change is not growth; as all movement is not forward.

—Ellen Glasgow

A bend in the road is not the end of the road ... Unless you fail to make the turn.

—Helen Keller

Just because everything is different doesn't mean everything has changed.

—Irene Peter

The wise adapt themselves to circumstances, as water moulds itself to the pitcher.

—Chinese proverb

We must sail sometimes with the wind and sometimes against it —but we must sail, and not drift, nor lie at anchor.

—Oliver Wendell Holmes, Jr.

Life is like the moon: now full, now dark.

— Polish proverb

Don't try to understand everything, because sometimes it isn't meant to be understood, but to be accepted.

— Unknown

Acceptance doesn't mean resignation; it means understanding that something is what it is and that there's got to be a way through it.

— Michael J. Fox

When we are no longer able to change a situation, we are challenged to change ourselves.

— Victor Frankl

All things must change/To something new, to something strange.
— Henry Wadsworth Longfellow

Adaptability is about the powerful difference between adapting to cope and adapting to win.

— Max McKeown

We delight in the beauty of the butterfly, but rarely admit the changes it has gone through to achieve that beauty.

— Maya Angelou

Just when the caterpillar thought the world was over, it became a butterfly.

— Unknown

The wings of transformation are born of patience and struggle.
— Janet S. Dickens

CHALLENGES MAKE US STRONGER, RIGHT?

It is not in the still calm of life, or the repose of a pacific station, that great characters are formed. The habits of a vigorous mind are formed in contending with difficulties.

—Abigail Adams

In the middle of every difficulty lies opportunity.

—Albert Einstein

The merit of all things lies in their difficulty.

—Alexandre Dumas

A problem is a chance for you to do your best.

—Duke Ellington

You can be shaped, or you can be broken. There is not much in between.

—David Foster Wallace

To be tested is good. The challenged life may be the best therapist.

—Gail Sheehy

Challenges make you discover things about yourself that you never really knew.

—Cicely Tyson

Don't limit your challenges. Challenge your limits.

—Unknown

Instead of thinking outside the box, get out of the box.

—Deepak Chopra

Courage comes while we are facing challenges and because we are facing challenges! Courage takes our hand as we step up.

— C. Cooper

The best thing one can do when it's raining is to let it rain.

— Henry Wadsworth Longfellow

Happiness is not the absence of problems, but the ability to deal with them.

— Charles De Montesquieu

Mountains cannot be surmounted except by winding paths.

— Johann Wolfgang Von Goethe

It's natural to be upset when faced with hardship. But try to pull yourself together. Your efforts won't go to waste.

— Mufti Menk

When we least expect it, life sets us a challenge to test our courage and willingness to change; at such a moment, there is no point in pretending that nothing has happened or in saying that we are not yet ready. The challenge will not wait. Life does not look back.

— Paulo Coelho

Smooth seas do not make skilled sailors.

— African proverb

And once the storm is over, you won't remember how you made it through, how you managed to survive. You won't even be sure, whether the storm is really over. But one thing is certain. When you come out of the storm, you won't be the same person who walked in. That's what this storm's all about.

— Haruki Murakami

The most beautiful people I've known are those who have known trials, have known struggles, have known loss, and have found their way out of the depths.

— Elisabeth Kübler-Ross

When faced with a challenge, look for a way, not a way out.

— David Weatherford

Your character is formed by the challenges you face and over-come.

—Nick Vucicic, *Unstoppable*

Don't get hung up on the hard times, the challenges. Tell your story by highlighting the victories. Because it's your victories that will inspire, motivate, encourage other people to live their stories in grander ways.

—Iyanla Vanzant

It is when I struggle that I strengthen. It is when challenged to my core that I learn the depth of who I am.

—Steve Maraboli

If you are going through hell, keep going.

—Winston Churchill

The most challenging times bring us the most empowering les-sons.

—Karen Salmansohn

God gave burdens, but he also gave shoulders.

—Yiddish proverb

I'm not afraid of storms, for I'm learning to sail my ship.

—Louisa May Alcott

It's gonna be a long hard drag, but we'll make it.

—Janis Joplin

The momentary challenges, the delays, the minor frustrations of this day will yield great benefit in the future, if only we learn to remain strong and peaceful through them.

—Joshua DuBois, *The President's Devotional*

Normality is a paved road. It's comfortable to walk on, but no flowers grow on it.

—Vincent van Gogh

Challenges are what make life interesting. Overcoming them is what makes them meaningful.

—Unknown

You can't smooth the surf, but you can learn to ride the waves.

—Unknown

Life is at its best when everything has fallen out of place, and you decide that you're going to fight to get them right, not when everything is going your way and everyone is praising you.

—Thisuri Wanniarachchi

There are some things you learn best in calm, and some in a storm.

—Willa Cather

Never try to solve all the problems at once — make them line up for you one-by-one.

—Richard Sloma

Hard times don't create heroes. It is during the hard times when the 'hero' within us is revealed.

—Unknown

The harder the conflict, the more glorious the triumph.

—Thomas Paine

People say nothing is impossible, but I do nothing every day.

—A.A. Milne, *Winnie the Pooh*

I believe in the impossible because no one else does.

—Florence Griffith Joyner

Start by doing what's necessary; then do what's possible; and suddenly you are doing the impossible.

—Francis of Assisi

It always seems impossible until it's done.

—Nelson Mandela

FLEXIBILITY: ADJUSTING ALONG THE WAY

The human capacity for burden is like bamboo — far more flexible than you'd ever believe at first glance.

—Jodi Picoult, *My Sister's Keeper*

Blessed are the flexible for they will not allow themselves to become bent out of shape!

—Robert Ludlum

The art of life lies in a constant readjustment to our surroundings.

—Kakuzo Okakura

Be flexible, but stick to your principles.

—Eleanor Roosevelt

Flexibility makes buildings to be stronger; imagine what it can do to your soul.

—Carlos Barrios

The most useful virtues, for one who walked on, were flexibility and a willingness to improvise.

—Rachel Hartman, *Tess of the Road*

What is malleable is always superior to that which is immovable. This is the principle of controlling things by going along with them, of mastery through adaptation.

—Lao Tzu

Be infinitely flexible and constantly amazed.

—Jason Kravits

ADVERSITY: LOOKING AT IT ANOTHER WAY

Adversity is like a strong wind. It tears away from us all but the things that cannot be torn, so that we see ourselves as we really are.

— Arthur Golden, *Memoirs of a Geisha*

Life is thickly sown with thorns, and I know no other remedy than to pass quickly through them. The longer we dwell on our misfortunes, the greater is their power to harm us.

— Voltaire

He knows not his own strength that hath not met adversity.

— Ben Jonson

If we had no winter, the spring would not be so pleasant: if we did not sometimes taste of adversity, prosperity would not be so welcome.

— Anne Bradstreet

There is no education like adversity.

— Benjamin Disraeli

Adversity has the effect of eliciting talents which, in prosperous circumstances, would have lain dormant.

— Horace

If we will be quiet and ready enough, we shall find compensation in every disappointment.

— Henry David Thoreau

The true course of any thing never does run smooth.

— Samuel Butler

When the winds of adversity blow strong, redirect their force into the service of your highest intention.

—Jonathan Lockwood Huie

You never really know what's coming. A small wave, or maybe a big one. All you can really do is hope that when it comes, you can surf over it, instead of drown in its monstrosity.

—Alysha Speer

You do learn how to cope from those who are coping.

—Matthew Desmond

The depth of the feeling continued to surprise and threaten me, but each time it hit again and I bore it...I would discover that it hadn't washed me away.

—Anne Lamott, *Traveling Mercies: Some Thoughts on Faith*

CARING: IT'S WHAT YOU DO

Care is a state in which something does matter; it is the source of human tenderness.

— Rollo May

Have a heart that never hardens, a temper that never tires, and a touch that never hurts.

— Charles Dickens

The capacity to care is the thing which gives life its deepest significance.

— Pablo Casals

The simple act of caring is heroic.

— Edward Albert

Love isn't a state of perfect caring. It is an active noun like struggle. To love someone is to strive to accept that person exactly the way he or she is, right here and now."

— Fred Rogers

We change the world when we simply meet the needs of another.
— Kristen Welch

If you find it in your heart to care for somebody else, you will have succeeded.

— Maya Angelou

To make a difference in someone's world, you don't have to be amazing, rich, talented, beautiful or perfect. You just have to be you and care.

— Rebecca Fox

No one is useless in this world who lightens the burdens of another.

— Charles Dickens

Not everyone will have the heart you have. Not everyone will appreciate you and what you do for them. Sometimes it won't be easy having a kind heart in a cruel world. Be prepared.

— Tony Gaskins

You care so much you feel as though you will bleed to death with the pain of it.

— J.K. Rowling

Live simply. Love generously. Care deeply. Speak kindly.

— Unknown

Gift the love of your life with undistracted, untelevisioned, un-hurried attentiveness.

— Mary Anne Radmacher

When we're together, paying attention is the most basic and pro-found expression of love — in a moment when you offer atten-tion, real listening, real presence — in that moment, the heart naturally opens. This is the most basic training in awakening our hearts: Mindful attention. Just being there.

— Tarah Brach

The most precious gift we can offer others is our presence. When mindfulness embraces those we love, they will bloom like flowers.

— Thich Nhat Hanh

Some people care too much. I think it's called love.

— A.A. Milne, *Winnie the Pooh*

Unless someone like you cares a whole awful lot, nothing is going to get better. It's not.

— Dr. Seuss

Do you wish to rise? Begin by descending. You plan a tower that will pierce the clouds? Lay first the foundation of humility.

— Augustine of Hippo

Humility is attentive patience.

— Simone Weil

COMPASSION: THE HEART OF GIVING CARE

The purpose of human life is to serve, and to show compassion and the will to help others.

— Albert Schweitzer

If you want others to be happy, practice compassion. If you want to be happy, practice compassion.

— Dalai Lama XIV

Tolerance and compassion are qualities of fearless people.

— Paulo Coelho

Simply let experience take place very freely so that your open heart is suffused with the tenderness of true compassion.

— Tsoknyi Rinpoche

Compassion isn't about solutions. It's about giving all the love that you've got.

— Cheryl Strayed

Compassion hurts. When you feel connected to everything, you also feel responsible for everything. And you cannot turn away. Your destiny is bound with the destinies of others. You must either learn to carry the Universe or be crushed by it. You must grow strong enough to love the world, yet empty enough to sit down at the same table with its worst horrors.
— Andrew Boyd, *Daily Afflictions: The Agony of Being Connected to Everything in the Universe*

Compassion is the wish to see others free from suffering.

— Dalai Lama XIV

One of the secrets of inner peace is the practice of compassion.

— Dalai Lama XIV

Compassion is to look beyond your own pain, to see the pain of others.

—Yasmin Mogahed

The whole idea of compassion is based on a keen awareness of the interdependence of all these living beings, which are all part of one another, and all involved in one another.

—Thomas Merton

for there is nothing heavier than compassion. Not even one's own pain weighs so heavy as the pain one feels with someone, for someone, a pain intensified by the imagination and prolonged by a hundred echoes.

—Milan Kundera, *The Unbearable Lightness of Being*

Compassion can be defined in many ways, but its essence is a basic kindness, with a deep awareness of the suffering of oneself and of other living things, coupled with the wish and effort to relieve it.

—Paul Gilbert, *The Compassionate Mind*

A sympathetic person is one who's motivated by compassion. Compassion is concern for the sufferings or misfortunes of others. It is the feeling that arises when you are confronted with another's suffering and feel motivated to relieve that suffering. Be sympathetic, be compassionate & live a meaningful life.

—Dr. Anil Kumar Sinha

The path of compassion is cultivated one step and one moment at a time.

—Christina Feldman

Compassion is not a relationship between the healer and the wounded. It's a relationship between equals. Only when we know our own darkness well, can we be present with the darkness of others. Compassion becomes real when we recognize our shared humanity.

—Pema Chödrön

Become a compassionate center rather becoming a diverting road.

— Agatha Fauvel, *Letting Go*

WORRY & FEAR: DO SOMETHING ANYWAY

Worry is an addiction that interferes with compassion.

— Deng Ming-Dao

That the birds of worry and care fly over your head, this you cannot change, but that they build nests in your hair, this you can prevent.

— Chinese proverb

What worries you, masters you.

— John Locke

All forms of fear produce fatigue.

— Bertrand Russell

How very little can be done under the spirit of fear.

— Florence Nightingale

We have to continually be jumping off cliffs and developing our wings on the way down.

— Kurt Vonnegut

The most drastic, and usually the most effective, remedy for fear is direct action.

— William Burnham

Become so wrapped up in something that you forget to be afraid.

— Lady Bird Johnson

Life begins where fear ends.

— Osho

Fear defeats more people than any other one thing in the world.

— Ralph Waldo Emerson

He has not learned the lesson of life who does not every day surmount a fear.

> — Ralph Waldo Emerson

Things done well and with care exempt themselves from fear.
> — William Shakespeare, *Henry VIII*

COURAGE: FACE THE FACE

Courage is grace under pressure.

— Ernest Hemingway

From caring comes courage.

— Lao Tzu

the courage it took to get out of bed each morning to face the same things over and over was enormous.
— Charles Bukowski, *You Get So Alone at Times That it Just Makes Sense*

Courage is not the absence of fear, but rather the judgment that something else is more important than fear.

— Ambrose Redmoon

Life shrinks or expands in proportion to one's courage.

— Anaïs Nin

Facing it, always facing it, that's the way to get through. Face it.

— Conrad Joseph

Courage consists not in blindly overlooking danger, but in seeing it and conquering it.

— Jean Paul Richter

With courage you will dare to take risks, have the strength to be compassionate, and the wisdom to be humble. Courage is the foundation of integrity.

— Keshavan Nair

When you have no choice, mobilize the spirit of courage.

— Jewish proverb

You have plenty of courage, I am sure," answered Oz. "All you need is confidence in yourself. There is no living thing that is not afraid when it faces danger. The true courage is in facing danger when

you are afraid, and that kind of courage you have in plenty.
— L. Frank Baum, *The Wonderful Wizard of Oz*

Courage does not always roar. Sometimes courage is the quite voice at the end of the day saying, 'I will try again tomorrow.'
— Mary Anne Radmacher

I am not a courageous person by nature. I have simply discovered that, at certain key moments in this life, you must find courage in yourself, in order to move forward and live. It is like a muscle and it must be exercised, first a little, and then more and more. All the really exciting things possible during the course of a lifetime require a little more courage than we currently have. A deep breath and a leap.
— John Patrick Shanley, *13 by Shanley*

You cannot swim for new horizons until you have courage to lose sight of the shore.

— William Faulkner

We got to fight the fight
We got to fall the falls
We got to light the light
We got to call the calls
Try to place the place
Where we can face the face.
We got to face the face...

— Pete Townshend - *"Face The Face"*

We don't develop courage by being happy every day. We develop it by surviving difficult times and challenging adversity.
— Barbara De Angelis

Promise me you'll always remember: You are braver than you believe, and stronger than you seem, and smarter than you think.
— A.A. Milne, *Winnie the Pooh*

Courage. Kindness. Friendship. Character. These are the qualities that define us as human beings, and propel us, on occasion, to

Craig Hlas

greatness.

— R.J. Palacio, *Wonder*

SACRIFICE: YOU GIVE YOURSELF AWAY

Giving yourself is the ultimate revolution.

— Bryan McGill

No man knows the genuineness of his convictions until he has sacrificed something for them.

— E.H. Chapin

All great things worth having require great sacrifice worth giving.

— Paulina Simons

The most sublime act is to set another before you.

— William Blake

Someday you will find out that there is far more happiness in another's happiness than in your own. It is something that I cannot explain, something within that sends a glow of warmth all through you.

— Honoré de Balzac, *Pere Goriot*

The sacrifice which causes sorrow to the doer of the sacrifice is no sacrifice. Real sacrifice lightens the mind of the doer and gives him a sense of peace and joy. The Buddha gave up the pleasures of life because they had become painful to him.

— Mahatma Gandhi

Life becomes harder for us when we live for others, but it also becomes richer and happier.

— Zahid Abas

Let the rest do whatever, while you do whatever it takes.

— Grant Cardone

Sacrifice is a part of life. It's supposed to be. It's not something to regret. It's something to aspire to. Little sacrifices. Big sacrifices.

Craig Hlas

A mother works so her son can go to school. A daughter moves home to take care of her sick father.
— Mitch Albom, *The Five People You Meet in Heaven*

SELFLESSNESS: LIGHTING ANOTHER CANDLE

Love is selfless. The key is giving up yourself.

—Zac Hanson

A candle loses nothing by lighting another candle.

—James Keller

It's when you're acting selflessly that you're at your bravest.

—Veronica Roth

Real living is living for others.

—Bruce Lee

I've learned that selflessness is a practice, not a place; a journey much more than a destination.

—Kayla Mueller

Our compassion and acts of selflessness take us to the deeper truths.

—Mata Amritanandamayi

Selfless service alone gives the needed strength and courage to awaken the sleeping humanity in one's heart.

—Sai Baba

Selfless giving doesn't mean you let people walk all over you.

—Frederick Lenz

Day after day, ordinary people become heroes through extraordinary and selfless actions.

—Sylvia Mathews Burwell

A hero is somebody who is selfless. Who is generous in spirit. Who just tries to give back as much as possible and help people. A hero to me is someone who saves people and who really deeply cares.

Craig Hlas

— Debi Mazar

DEPENDABLE & DEDICATED: INSPIRING CONFIDENCE

A person who inspires confidence is one who carries a fine attitude. Wholesome attitude radiates trust, and trust is that quality of life that is fundamental in dependability, and dependability is more to be desired than a brilliant mind.

—Joseph Quinney Jr.

Dependability is the base upon which all confidence rests in full security. Confidence may be termed the active result of basic dependability.

—Robert E. Hicks

And the strongest trust is built by the smallest actions, the keeping of the little promises. It is the constant truthfulness, the continued dependability, the remembrance of minor things, which most inspire confidence and faith.

—Walter Wangerin Jr.

Dependability is sincerity plus willpower. Dependability is merely an outcropping of character.

—Roy L. Smith

There is no chance, no destiny, no fate, that can hinder or control the firm resolve of a determined soul.

—Ella Wheeler Wilcox

Above all be of single aim; have a legitimate and useful purpose, and devote yourself unreservedly to it.

—James Allen

Dedicate some of your life to others. Your dedication will not be a sacrifice. It will be an exhilarating experience because it is an intense effort applied toward a meaningful end.

—Dr. Thomas Dooley

Dedication is not what others expect of you, it is what you can give to others.

—Unknown

Risk more than others think is safe. Care more than others think is wise. Dream more than others think is practical. Expect more than others think is possible.

—Claude Bissel

If the sky that we look upon
Should tumble and fall
Or the mountains should crumble to the sea
I won't cry, I won't cry, no I won't shed a tear
Just as long as you stand, stand by me

—Ben E. King – "Stand By Me"

DETERMINATION: SHINING FOR ANOTHER

You gain strength, courage, and confidence by every experience in which you really stop to look fear in the face. You must do the things which you think you cannot do.

— Eleanor Roosevelt

When you get to the end of your rope, tie a knot and hang on.

— Franklin D. Roosevelt

Either I will find a way, or I will make one.

— Philip Sidney

Beginning is easy; continuing, hard.

— Japanese proverb

Anyone can give up; it's the easiest thing in the world to do. But to hold it together when everyone would expect you to fall apart, that's true strength.

— Chris Bradford

The block of granite which is an obstacle in the pathway of the weak becomes a stepping stone in the pathway of the strong.

— Unknown

It is not the mountain we conquer but ourselves.

— Edmund Hillary

If you can't fly then run, if you can't run, then walk, if you can't walk then crawl, but whatever you do you have to keep moving forward.

— Martin Luther King Jr.

I have learned over the years that when one's mind is made up, this diminishes fear; knowing what must be done does away with fear.

>   — Rosa Parks

Courage and perseverance have a magical talisman, before which
difficulties disappear and obstacles vanish into air.
>   — John Quincy Adams

Determination that just won't quit — that's what it takes.
>   — A.J. Foyt

When the sky is grey
Hope just hides away
I'll be your sunflower
When you can't stand up
Even love is not enough
I'll be your sunflower
I shine for you
You know I'd do
Anything for you

>   — The Weepies - *Sunflower*

PERSEVERE & PERSIST: ONE SMALL RACE AT A TIME

Perseverance is not a long race; it is many short races one after another.

— Walter Elliott, *The Spiritual Life*

Perseverance is the ability to keep going in the face of continuous challenges. It is the ability to disregard distractions and to stay focused.

— Catherine Pulsifer

I think a hero is an ordinary individual who finds strength to persevere and endure in spite of overwhelming obstacles.

— Christopher Reeve

I will breathe. I will think of solutions. I will not let my worry control me. I will not let my stress level break me. I will simply breathe. And it will be okay. Because I don't quit.

— Shane McLendon

Whenever you find yourself doubting how far you can go, just remember how far you have come. Remember everything you have faced, all the battles you have won, and all the fears you have overcome.

— Unknown

You may be sad, disappointed, heartbroken or even scarred. But wake each day with a new sense of hope, a will to fight on and not give up.

— Unknown

To persevere, trusting in what hopes he has, is courage in a man. The coward despairs.

— Euripides

Hard times ain't quit and we ain't quit.

— Meridel Le Sueur

One can go a long way after one is tired.

— French proverb

It isn't hard to be good from time to time. ... What's tough is being good every day.

— Willie Mays

It does not matter how slowly you go so long as you do not stop.

— Confucius

Life is not easy for any of us. But what of that? We must have perseverance and above all confidence in ourselves. We must believe that we are gifted for something and that this thing must be attained.

— Marie Curie

The best way out is always through.

— Robert Frost

Permanence, perseverance, and persistence in spite of all obstacles, discouragements, and impossibilities: It is this, that in all things distinguishes the strong soul from the weak.

— Thomas Carlyle

When you have exhausted all possibilities, remember this: You haven't.

— Thomas Edison

Don't look back. You're not going that way.

— Unknown

I didn't come this far to only go this far.

— Unknown

Perseverance, secret of all triumphs.

— Victor Hugo

HOPE: A LITTLE CAN GO
A LONG WAY

We must accept finite disappointment, but never lose infinite hope.

>—Martin Luther King Jr.

Hope is the thing with feathers that perches in the soul — and sings the tunes without the words — and never stops at all.

>—Emily Dickinson

Where there is no hope, it is incumbent on us to invent it.

>—Albert Camus

Life begins on the other side of despair.

>—Jean-Paul Sartre

Only in the darkness can you see the stars.

>—Dr. Martin Luther King, Jr.

Hope begins in the dark, the stubborn hope that if you just show up and try to do the right thing, the dawn will come. You wait and watch and work; you don't give up.

>—Anne Lamott

In the midst of gathering darkness, light becomes more evident.

>—Bonnie Bostrom

Hope is being able to see that there is light despite all of the darkness.

>—Desmond Tutu

Even the darkest night will end and the sun will rise.

>—Victor Hugo

However long the night, the dawn will break.

>—African proverb (Hausa tribe)

There is no hope unmingled with fear, and no fear unmingled with hope.

— Baruch de Spinoza

Hope is outreaching desire with expectancy of good. It is a characteristic of all living beings.

— Edward S. Ame

Clouds come floating into my life, no longer to carry rain or usher storm, but to add color to my sunset sky.

— Rabindranath Tagore

Carve a tunnel of hope through the dark mountain of disappointment.

— Martin Luther King Jr

Hope is the first thing to take some sort of action.

— John Armstrong

No hope, no action.

— Peter Levi

Find the seed at the bottom of your heart and bring forth a flower.

— Shigenori Kameoka

I dwell in possibility.

— Emily Dickinson

I always entertain great hopes.

— Robert Frost

So you could use a little, use a little
Leave it when you've done it
And I won't let go
'Cause with a little, with a little it can go a long way
Hoooo-ope hooooo-ope, hoooo-ope
I've got hope

Natasha Bedingfield - *Hope*

Hope means hoping when things are hopeless, or it is no virtue at all… As long as matters are really hopeful, hope is mere flattery or platitude; it is only when everything is hopeless that hope begins to be a strength.

—G.K. Chesterton

Once you choose hope, anything is possible.

—Christopher Reeve

Hang on to your hat. Hang on to your hope. And wind the clock, for tomorrow is another day.

—E.B. White

Give me hope
Help me cope, with this heavy load
Trying to, touch and reach you with,
heart and soul

—George Harrison – *"Give Me Love"*

LISTENING: TAKE IN EVERY STORY

When we want to talk, we can instead listen, and let our attentiveness to another's need to speak be our silent statement.

— Bryant H. McGill

Listening is a magnetic and strange thing, a creative force. The friends who listen to us are the ones we move toward. When we are listened to, it creates us, makes us unfold and expand.

— Karl A. Menniger

You cannot truly listen to anyone and do anything else at the same time.

— M. Scott Peck

The first duty of love is to listen.

— Paul Tillich

I need to listen well so that I hear what is not said.

— Thuli Madonsela

The most important thing in communication is hearing what isn't said.

— Peter Drucker

The quieter you become, the more you are able to hear.

— Rumi

One of the most valuable things we can do to heal one another is listen to each other's stories.

— Rebecca Falls

I'd be so happy to hear those voices again. ... You can find the most amazing stories from regular people. All you have to do is ask them about their lives and listen.

—Dave Isay, *Listening Is an Act of Love: A StoryCorps Special*

When we ground ourselves in the present moment, we spontaneously connect better with others. We become more responsive and less reactive, listening more deeply and speaking with greater clarity.
—Lama Surya Das, *Buddha Standard Time: Awakening to the Infinite Possibilities of Now*

When people talk, listen completely. Most people never listen.
— Ernest Hemingway

Listen with curiosity. Speak with honesty. Act with integrity. The greatest problem with communication is we don't listen to understand. We listen to reply. When we listen with curiosity, we don't listen with the intent to reply. We listen for what's behind the words.
— Roy T. Bennett, *The Light in the Heart*

EMPATHY: GETTING IN TUNE WITH ANOTHER

Empathy is simply listening, holding space, withholding judgment, emotionally connecting, and communicating that incredibly healing message of you're not alone.

— Brené Brown

A prerequisite to empathy is simply paying attention to the person in pain.

— Daniel Goleman

Empathy is full presence to what's alive in the other person at this moment.

— John Cunningham

Empathy is seeing with the eyes of another, listening with the ears of another, and feeling with the heart of another.

— Unknown

Any man filled with empathy is capable of gaining valuable insights on the human condition through the suffering of others. You do not need to suffer to know suffering, but you need empathy first to identify and feel the suffering of others around you.
— Suzy Kassem, *Rise Up and Salute the Sun*

Empathy isn't just something that happens to us — a meteor shower of synapses firing across the brain — it's also a choice we make: to pay attention, to extend ourselves. It's made of exertion, that dowdier cousin of impulse. Sometimes we care for another because we know we should, or because it's asked for, but this doesn't make our caring hollow.
— Leslie Jamison, *The Empathy Exams: Essays*

Because of your difficult experience, you will become stronger, wiser and more compassionate toward those having a hard time.

—Haemin Sunim

You can only understand people if you feel them in yourself.

—John Steinbeck

Empathy is formed through immersion.

—Jon Kolko

Resolve to be tender with the young, compassionate with the aged, sympathetic with the striving, and tolerant of the weak and the wrong. Sometime in life you will have been all of these

—George Washington Carver

Anguish is the universal language.

—Alice Fulton

May we always be burdened with thinking of the suffering of others, for that is what it means to be human.

—Kamand Kojouri

Our bodies have five senses: touch, smell, taste, sight, hearing. But not to be overlooked are the senses of our souls: intuition, peace, foresight, trust, empathy. The differences between people lie in their use of these senses; most people don't know anything about the inner senses while a few people rely on them just as they rely on their physical senses, and in fact probably even more.

—C. Joybell C.

Empathy requires knowing that you know nothing.

—Leslie Jamison

I think people believe empathy to be compassion, that compassion is an inner sense (a sense of the soul). But empathy is a sense, while compassion isn't a sense. Empathy is an affinity, a communion, a comprehension.

—C. Joybell C.

I call him religious who understands the suffering of others.

—Mahatma Gandhi

All I ever wanted was to reach out and touch another human being not just with my hands but with my heart.

— Tahereh Mafi

Sometimes all a person wants is an empathetic ear; all he or she needs is to talk it out. Just offering a listening ear and an understanding heart for his or her suffering can be a big comfort.

— Roy T. Bennett

If we can share our story with someone who responds with empathy and understanding, shame can't survive.

— Brené Brown, *Daring Greatly*

One of the most important things you can do on this earth is to let people know they are not alone.

— Shannon L. Alder

I do not ask the wounded person how he feels, I myself become the wounded person.

— Walt Whitman

UNDERSTANDING: A DEEPER KNOWING

The most beautiful people we have known are those who have known defeat, known suffering, known struggle, known loss, and have found their way out of the depths. These persons have an appreciation, a sensitivity, and an understanding of life that fills them with compassion, gentleness, and a deep loving concern. Beautiful people do not just happen.

—Elisabeth Kübler-Ross

All, everything that I understand, I understand only because I love.

—Leo Tolstoy

Any fool can know. The point is to understand.

—Albert Einstein

there's nothing more intimate in life than simply being understood. And understanding someone else.

—Brad Meltzer, *The Inner Circle*

How many things have to happen to you before something occurs to you?

—Robert Frost

How much can we ever know about the love and pain in another heart? How much can we hope to understand those who have suffered deeper anguish, greater deprivation, and more crushing disappointments than we ourselves have known?

—Orhan Pamuk, *Snow*

SUPPORT: BEING THERE, LIFTING UP

Those who are happiest are those who do the most for others.
— Booker T. Washington

When a person is down in the world, an ounce of help is better than a pound of preaching.
— Edward G. Bulwer-Lytton

Call it a clan, call it a network, call it a tribe, call it a family. Whatever you call it, whoever you are, you need one.
— Jane Howard

He stands erect by bending over the fallen. He rises by lifting others.
— Robert Green Ingersoll

The truest help we can render an afflicted man is not to take his burden from him, but to call out his best energy, that he may be able to bear the burden.
— Phillips Brooks

Sometimes the only thing you could do for people was to be there.
— Terry Pratchett

It's a kingly act to assist the fallen.
— Ovid

It is not enough to help the feeble up, but to support him after.
— William Shakespeare, *Timon of Athens*

Be strong, be fearless, be beautiful. And believe that anything is possible when you have the right people there to support you.
— Misty Copeland

Was it you or I who stumbled first? It does not matter. The one of us who finds the strength to get up first, must help the other.
　　　　　— Vera Nazarian, *The Perpetual Calendar of Inspiration*

When you're weak, I'll be strong
When you let go, I'll hold on
When you need to cry, I swear
That I'll be there to dry your eyes
When you feel lost and scared to death,
Like you can't take one more step
Just take my hand, together we can do it
I'm gonna love you through it.
　　　　　— Martina McBride – *"I'm Gonna Love You Through It"*

LAUGHTER: TAKE YOUR MEDICINE

Laughter can relieve tension in even the heaviest of matters.

— Allen Klein

The most wasted of all days is one without laughter.

— e.e. cummings

A good laugh and a long sleep are the two best cures for anything.

— Irish proverb

Laughter is an instant vacation.

— Milton Berle

Laughter is the closest distance between two people.

— Victor Borge

At the height of laughter, the universe is flung into a kaleidoscope of new possibilities.

— Jean Houston

Laughter and tears are both responses to frustration and exhaustion. I prefer to laugh, since there is less cleaning up to do afterwards.

— Kurt Vonnegut

Always laugh when you can. It is cheap medicine.

— Lord Byron

Against the assault of laughter nothing can stand.

— Mark Twain

The human race has one really effective weapon, and that is laughter.

— Mark Twain

I like the laughter that opens the lips and the heart, that shows at the same time, pearls of the mind.

—Victor Hugo

Laughter is the sun that drives winter from the human face.

—Victor Hugo

Laugher is the tonic, the relief, the surcease for pain.

—Charlie Chaplin

ENCOURAGEMENT GOES A LONG WAY

Most of us, swimming against the tides of trouble the world knows nothing about, need only a bit of praise or encouragement —and we will make the goal.

—Jerome Fleishman

Instruction does much, but encouragement everything.

—Johann Wolfgang von Goethe

Everyone has inside them a piece of good news. The good news is you don't know how great you can be! How much you can love! What you can accomplish! And what your potential is.

—Anne Frank

Encourage, lift and strengthen one another. For the positive energy spread to one will be felt by us all. For we are connected, one and all.

—Deborah Day

Put yourself in a state of mind where you say to yourself, Here is an opportunity for me to celebrate like never before, my own power, my own ability to get myself to do whatever is necessary.

—Dr. Martin Luther King

Just don't give up what you're trying to do. Where there is love and inspiration, I don't think you can go wrong.

—Ella Fitzgerald

Always try to keep a patch of sky above your life.

—Marcel Proust

As your faith is strengthened, you will find that there is no longer the need to have a sense of control, that things will flow as they will, and that you will flow with them, to your great delight and benefit.

—Emmanuel

Never give up, for that is just the place and time that the tide will turn.

—Harriet Beecher Stowe

Heaven is under our feet, as well as over our heads.

—Henry David Thoreau

It is by going down into the abyss that we recover the treasures of life. Where you stumble, there lies your treasure.

—Joseph Campbell

There is nothing better than the encouragement of a good friend.

—Katharine Butler Hathaway

When you encourage others, you in the process are encouraged because you're making a commitment and difference in that person's life. Encouragement really does make a difference.

—Zig Ziglar

Turn your face to the sun and the shadows fall behind you.

—Maori proverb

Life is a shipwreck but we must not forget to sing in the lifeboats.

—Voltaire

Taking an interest in what others are thinking and doing is often a much more powerful form of encouragement than praise.

—Robert Martin

Be like the bird that, passing on her flight awhile on boughs too slight, feels them give way beneath her, and yet sings, knowing that she hath wings.

—Victor Hugo

ENTHUSIASM KEEPS YOUR
MISSION IN MOTION

Enthusiasm will steady the heart and strengthen the will; it will give force to the thought and nerve to the hand until what was only a possibility becomes a reality.

—Orison Swett Marden

Enthusiasm is the mother of effort, and without it nothing great was ever achieved.

—Ralph Waldo Emerson

Nothing was ever achieved without enthusiasm.

—Henry David Thoreau

Nothing is so contagious as enthusiasm.

—Samuel Taylor Coleridge

Enthusiasm is excitement with inspiration, motivation, and a pinch of creativity.

—Bo Bennett

Enthusiasm is the yeast that rises the dough.

—Paul J. Meyer

The enthusiastic person will find ways around any setbacks, they may fall down, but they are quick to stand up again.

—Catherine Pulsifer

When you discover your mission, you will feel its demand. It will fill you with enthusiasm and a burning desire to get to work on it.

—W. Clement Stone

The secret of genius is to carry the spirit of the child into old age, which means never losing your enthusiasm.

—Aldous Huxley

Enthusiasm is everything. It must be taut and vibrating like a guitar string.

— Pelé

Indeed, there is an eloquence in true enthusiasm that is not to be doubted.

— Edgar Allan Poe

Then there is a still higher type of courage — the courage to brave pain, to live with it, to never let others know of it and to still find joy in life; to wake up in the morning with an enthusiasm for the day ahead.

— Howard Cosell

The dictionary defines enthusiasm as having 'intense and eager enjoyment, interest, or approval' for something. I tweak it a bit by defining enthusiasm as sustaining high energy with a positive anticipation for what's about to take place.

— John Baskin, *Simple And Effective Strategies On How To Create More Enthusiasm For Life*

PESSIMISM DOESN'T GET IT DONE

Pessimism becomes a self-fulfilling prophecy; it reproduces itself by crippling our willingness to act.

—Howard Zinn

I'm a pessimist because of intelligence, but an optimist because of will.

—Antonio Gramsci

A pessimist sees the difficulty in every opportunity; an optimist sees the opportunity in every difficulty.

—Winston Churchill

The pessimist complains about the wind; the optimist expects it to change; the realist adjusts the sails.

—William Arthur Ward

The optimist's hope and the pessimist's despair: reciprocal illusions.

—Marty Rubin

Some people are optimists. Some people are pessimists. I'm just a realist who believes that some things are worth fighting for.

—C. Joybell C.

Man stands in his own shadow and wonders why it's dark.

—Zen proverb

POSITIVE & OPTIMISTIC: LIGHT THE WAY

Positivity will block the negative thoughts that overwhelm you during tough times. Stay positive and you'll achieve more than what you set yourself for.

— Anurag Prakash Ray

By choosing positivity you become a contender for the human spirit giving hope to those in need.

— Bryant McGill

Believe you can and you're halfway there.

— Theodore Roosevelt

Staying positive does not mean that things will turn out okay. Rather it is knowing that YOU will be okay no matter how things turn out.

— Unknown

Give light and people will find the way.

— Ella Baker

A single sunbeam can drive away many shadows.

— St. Francis of Assisi

I think I am going to have to supercharge my optimism to arm myself for the battle ahead. Trust me, it is going to be a battle.

— Rebecca Bloom

I have the ability to build myself up or break myself down. I stay positive. Strength comes from within.

— Hayley Williams

Be fanatically positive and militantly optimistic. If something is not to your liking, change your liking.

— Rick Steves

You need to have faith in yourself. Be brave and take risks. You don't have to have it all figured out to move forward.

          — Roy T. Bennett

Storm? Shine your light and make a rainbow.

          — Richie Norman

Dwell on the beauty of life. Watch the stars, and see yourself running with them.

      — Marcus Aurelius, *Meditations*

Hoping all the verses rhyme
And the very best of choruses to
Follow all the doubt and sadness
I know that better things are on their way
Here's hoping that the days ahead
Won't be as bitter as the ones behind you
Be an optimist instead

     — Fountains of Wayne – *"Better Days"*

LOVE

Being deeply loved by someone gives you strength, while loving someone deeply gives you courage.

—Lao Tsu

The measure of love is to love without measure.

—Saint Augustine

Love is the poetry of the senses.

—Honoré de Balzac

Love cures people — both the ones who give it and the ones who receive it.

—Karl Menninger

I love you with so much of my heart that none is left to protest.
—William Shakespeare, *Much Ado About Nothing*

Let your love be like the misty rain, coming softly but flooding the river.

—Liberian proverb

In family life, love is the oil that eases friction, the cement that binds closer together, and the music that brings harmony.

—Eva Burrows

Loving is the most unmitigated and courageous act I perform in a day.

—Mary Anne Radmacher

There is not as much accomplished without love as there is with it. The presence of love is the greatest method, manner, mode, agent, and tool of change that there is in the universe.

—Shannon Scott, *Regret*

The first duty of love is to listen.

—Paul Tillich

Each of us can learn the art of nourishing happiness and love. Everything needs food to live, even love. If we don't know how to nourish our love, it withers. When we feed and support our own happiness, we are nourishing our ability to love. That's why to love means to learn the art of nourishing our happiness.
> — Thich Nhat Hanh, *How to Love (Mindful Essentials)*

To be fully seen by somebody, then, and be loved anyhow – this is a human offering that can border on miraculous.
> — Elizabeth Gilbert

Piglet: 'How do you spell 'love'?' Winnie the Pooh: 'You don't spell it…you feel it.'"
> —A.A. Milne, *Winnie the Pooh*

GIVING YIELDS BRILLIANT, INTANGIBLE REWARDS

You can give without loving, but you cannot love without giving.
— Amy Carmichael

Love grows by giving. The love we give away is the only love we keep. The only way to retain love is to give it away.
— Elbert Hubbard

Give yourself entirely to those around you. Be generous with your blessings. A kind gesture can reach a wound that only compassion can heal.
— Steve Maraboli, *Life, the Truth, and Being Free*

The only gift is a portion of thyself.
— Ralph Waldo Emerson

Real generosity toward the future lies in giving all to the present.
— Albert Camus

You don't have to be an angel, just be someone who can give.
— Patti LaBelle, *Angel*

As we work to create light for others, we naturally light our own way.
— Mary Anne Radmacher

It is enough that I am of value to somebody today.
— Hugh Prather

Real unselfishness consists in sharing the interests of others.
— George Santayana

Thousands of candles can be lit from a single candle, and the life of the candle will not be shortened.
— Buddha

Learn to light a candle in the darkest moments of someone's life. Be the light that helps others see; it is what gives life its deepest significance.

—Roy T. Bennett, *The Light in the Heart*

Plant flowers in others' gardens and your life becomes a bouquet!

—Unknown

To share often and much... to know even one life has breathed easier because you have lived. This is to have succeeded.

—Ralph Waldo Emerson

Measure thy life by loss instead of gain/Not by the wine drunk, but by the wine poured forth.

—Harriet King

For it is in giving that we receive.

—Francis of Assisi

GENEROSITY IS SOUL EXPANDING

That's what I consider true generosity: You give your all, and yet you always feel as if it costs you nothing.

— Simone de Beauvoir

If truth doesn't set you free, generosity of spirit will.

— Katerina Stoykova Klemer

What comes from the heart, goes to the heart.

— Samuel Taylor Coleridge

What I call the depth of generosity is when people are very fond of giving away what they need most themselves.

— Oscar Wilde

To be able to practice five things everywhere under heaven constitutes perfect virtue...[They are] gravity, generosity of soul, sincerity, earnestness, and kindness.

— Confucius

Sometimes when we are generous in small, barely detectable ways it can change someone else's life forever.

— Margaret Cho

BEING & DOING GOOD,
SHORT OF PERFECTION

And now that you don't have to be perfect, you can be good.
—John Steinbeck, *East of Eden*

Goodness is the only investment that never fails.
—Henry David Thoreau

Goodness is about character — integrity, honesty, kindness, generosity, moral courage, and the like. More than anything else, it is about how we treat other people.
—Dennis Prager

Of all virtues and dignities of the mind, goodness is the greatest.
—Francis Bacon

Do all the good you can and make as little fuss as possible about it.
—Charles Dickens

Every man is guilty of all the good he did not do.
—Voltaire

Do your little bit of good where you are; it's those little bits of good put together that overwhelm the world.
—Desmond Tutu

With every deed you are sowing a seed, though the harvest you may not see.
—Ella Wheeler Wilcox

The unselfish effort to bring cheer to others will be the beginning of a happier life for ourselves.
—Helen Keller

Doing good to others is not a duty, it is a joy, for it increases our own health and happiness.

—Zoroaster

HELP & SERVE: ASK FOR IT, GIVE IT AWAY

Down in their hearts, wise men know this truth: the only way to help yourself is to help others.

— Elbert Hubbard

In helping others, we shall help ourselves, for whatever good we give out completes the circle and comes back to us.

— Flora Edwards

When a person is down in the world, an ounce of help is better than a pound of preaching.

— Edward George Bulwer-Lytton

We're here for a reason. I believe a bit of the reason is to throw little torches out to lead people through the dark.

— Whoopi Goldberg

It is one of the most beautiful compensations of this life that no man can sincerely try to help another without helping himself.

— Ralph Waldo Emerson

Great opportunities to help others seldom come, but small ones surround us every day.

— Sally Koch

Be strong enough to stand alone, smart enough to know when you need help, and brave enough to ask for it.

— Unknown

A man of humanity is one who...desiring attainment for himself, helps others to attain.

— Confucius

When you reach out to those in need, do not be surprised if the essential meaning of something occurs.

— Stephen Richards

I slept and dreamt that life was joy. I awoke and saw that life was service. I acted and behold, service was joy.

— Rabindranath Tagore

Service to others is the rent you pay for living on this planet.

— Marian Wright Edelman

Lose yourself in generous service and every day can be a most unusual day, a triumphant day, an abundantly rewarding day!

— William Arthur Ward

If you're lost you can look and you will find me
Time after time
If you fall I will catch you, I will be waiting
Time after time

— Cyndi Lauper – *"Time After Time"*

KINDNESS

No act of kindness, no matter how small, is ever wasted.

—Aesop

Guard well within yourself that treasure, kindness. Know how to give without hesitation, how to lose without regret, how to acquire without meanness.

—George Sand

A single act of kindness throws out roots in all directions, and the roots spring up and make new trees.

—Amelia Earhart

Kindness can transform someone's dark moment with a blaze of light. You'll never know how much your caring matters. Make a difference for another today.

—Amy Leigh Mercree

Tenderness is a virtue.

—Oliver Goldsmith

Kindness and a generous spirit go a long way.

—Max Irons

What wisdom can you find that is greater than kindness?

—Jean Jacques Rousseau

Kindness is the language which the deaf can hear and the blind can see.

—Mark Twain

True beauty is a warm heart, a kind soul, and an attentive ear.

—Ken Poirot

Nothing is so strong as gentleness, nothing so gentle as real strength.

—Saint Francis de Sales

Kindness in words creates confidence. Kindness in thinking creates profoundness. Kindness in giving creates love.

—Lao Tsu

Love and kindness go hand in hand.

—Marian Keyes

Getting money is not all a man's business: to cultivate kindness is a valuable part of the business of life.

—Samuel Johnson

Too often we underestimate the power of a touch, a smile, a kind word, a listening ear, an honest compliment, or the smallest act of caring, all of which have the potential to turn a life around.

—Leo Buscaglia

The kindest hearts have felt the most pains.

—Unknown

Life is short and we have never too much time for gladdening the hearts of those who are travelling the dark journey with us. Oh be swift to love, make haste to be kind.

—Henri Frederic Amiel

Kind hearts are the gardens. Kind thoughts are the roots. Kind words are the blossoms. Kind deeds are the fruits.

—Kirpal Singh

Kindness gives birth to kindness.

—Sophocles

I see their souls, and I hold them in my hands, and because I love them they weigh nothing.

—Pearl Bailey

To become acquainted with kindness one must be prepared to learn new things and feel new feelings. Kindness is more than a philosophy of the mind. It is a philosophy of the spirit.

—Robert J. Furey

A kind word is like a spring day.

—Russian proverb

Kindness makes you the most beautiful person in the world, no matter what you look like.

—Unknown

There's no such thing as a small act of kindness. Every act creates a ripple with no logical end.

—Scott Adams

Miss no single opportunity of making some small sacrifice, here by a smiling look, there by a kindly word; always doing the smallest right and doing it all for love.

—Saint Thérèse of Lisieux

Kindness in ourselves is the honey that blunts the sting of unkindness in another.

—Walter Savage Landor

How far that little candle throws his beams! So shines a good deed in a weary world.

—William Shakespeare, *Merchant of Venice*

A single sunbeam is enough to drive away many shadows.

—Francis of Assisi

That best portion of a good man's life, His little, nameless, unremembered acts of kindness and of love.
—William Wordsworth, *Lines Composed a Few Miles above Tintern Abbey*

I have understood that the most important things are tenderness and kindness. I can't do without them.

—Brigitte Bardot

There is an organic affinity between joyousness and tenderness, and their companionship in the saintly life need in no way occasion surprise.

—William James

Tenderness and kindness are not signs of weakness and despair, but manifestations of strength and resolution.

—Kahlil Gibran

The true meaning of life is to plant trees, under whose shade you do not expect to sit.

—Nelson Henderson

A laugh, to be joyous, must flow from a joyous heart, for without kindness, there can be no true joy.

—Thomas Carlyle

Act with kindness, but do not expect gratitude.

—Confucius

Deliberately seek opportunities for kindness, sympathy, and patience.

—Evelyn Underhill

FRIEND: RUNNING TOWARD
THE FIRE

The glory of friendship is not the outstretched hand, not the kindly smile, nor the joy of companionship; it is the spiritual inspiration that comes to one when you discover that someone else believes in you and is willing to trust you with a friendship.

> — Ralph Waldo Emerson

One of the most beautiful qualities of true friendship is to understand and to be understood.

> — Seneca

Friends show their love in times of trouble, not in happiness.

> — Euripides

Be more prompt to go to a friend in adversity than in prosperity.

> — Chilo

One's life has value so long as one attributes value to the life of others, by means of love, friendship, and compassion.

> — Simone de Beauvoir

As iron sharpens iron, so a friend sharpens a friend.

> — King Solomon

A friend is the one who comes in when the whole world has gone out.

> — Grace Pulpit

We are all travelers in the wilderness of this world, and the best we can find in our travels is an honest friend.

> — Robert Louis Stevenson

One of the tasks of true friendship is to listen compassionately and creatively to the hidden silences. Often secrets are not revealed in words, they lie concealed in the silence between the

words or in the depth of what is unsayable between two people.
—John O'Donohue

Friendship improves happiness and abates misery by doubling of our joy and the dividing of our grief.
— Marcus Cicero

And in this crazy life
And through these crazy times
It's you, it's you
You make me sing
You're every line
You're every word
You're everything

— Michael Bublé – *"Everything"*

THE HUMAN EXPERIENCE IS
NOT A MARKETING SLOGAN

You can make people feel valued or cared for by design alone. It's not purely about money. It's about how we choose to value human experience.

— Thomas Heatherwick

Remember, you don't live in a world all your own.

— Albert Schweitzer

Remember your humanity, and forget the rest.

— Bertrand Russell

Man is harder than rock and more fragile than an egg.

— Yugoslav proverb

Man is harder than iron, stronger than stone, and more fragile than a rose.

— Turkish proverb

The years teach much which the days never know.

— Ralph Waldo Emerson

All I have is a sense of duty toward all people and an attachment to those with whom I have become intimate.

— Albert Einstein

In recognizing the humanity of our fellow beings, we pay ourselves the highest tribute.

— Thurgood Marshall

We think too much and feel too little. More than machinery, we need humanity; more than cleverness, we need kindness and gentleness. Without these qualities, life will be violent and all will be lost.

— Charles Chaplin

We are very, very small, but we are profoundly capable of very, very big things.

—Stephen Hawking

LIFE: ONE AMAZING DAY
AT A TIME

To live is so startling it leaves little time for anything else.

— Emily Dickinson

Life is like riding a bicycle. To keep your balance, you must keep moving.

— Albert Einstein

Any idiot can face a crisis — it's this day-to-day living that wears you out.

— Anton Chekhov

Life is no "brief candle" for me. It is a sort of splendid torch, which I have got hold of for the moment; and I want to make it burn as brightly as possible before handing it on to future generations.

— George Bernard Shaw

We will be known forever by the tracks we leave.

— Dakota proverb

The most fortunate are those who have a wonderful capacity to appreciate again and again, freshly and naively, the basic goods of life, with awe, pleasure, wonder, and even ecstasy.

— Abraham H. Maslow

Life has many ways of testing a person's will, either by having nothing happen at all or by having everything happen at once.

— Paulo Coelho

A life spent worthily should be measured by deeds, not years.

— Richard Sheridan

Wholehearted living is about engaging in our lives from a place of worthiness. It means cultivating the courage, compassion, and connection to wake up in the morning and think, No matter what gets done and how much is left undone, I am enough.

—Brené Brown, *Daring Greatly*

Life does not accommodate you, it shatters you ... every seed destroys its container or else there would be no fruition.

—Florida Scott-Maxwell

Not everyone will understand your journey. That's fine. It's not their journey to make sense of. It's yours.

—Unknown

The purpose of life is not to be happy. It is to be useful, to be honorable, to be compassionate, to have it make some difference that you have lived and lived well.

—Ralph Waldo Emerson

The main thing is to be moved, to love, to hope, to tremble, to live.

—Auguste Rodin

The purpose of life is a life of purpose.

—Robert Byrne

All my life's a circle;
Sunrise and sundown;
Moon rolls through the nighttime;
'Til the daybreak comes around.

—Harry Chapin – *"Circle"*

PAIN & SUFFERING: SACRED TEARS, SPECIAL SOULS

Out of suffering have emerged the strongest souls; the most massive characters are seared with scars.

> — Edwin H. Chapin

You are so brave and quiet I forget you are suffering.

> — Ernest Hemingway

To hurt is as human as to breathe.

> — J.K. Rowling

When sorrows come they come not as single spies but in battalions.

> — William Shakespeare, *Hamlet*

I think that humans have a huge capacity to carry pain and sadness. There are things that haunt us our entire lives; we are unable to let them go. The good times seem almost effervescent and dreamlike in comparison with the times that didn't go so well.

> — Henry Rollins

Sometimes you must hurt in order to know, fall in order to grow, lose in order to gain, because life's greatest lessons are learnt through pain.

> — Nagato

That's the thing about pain, it demands to be felt.

> — John Green

There is prodigious strength in sorrow and despair.

> — Charles Dickens

Pain or love or danger makes you real again.

> — Jack Kerouac

The most glorious moments in your life are not the so-called days of success, but rather those days when out of dejection and despair you feel rise in you a challenge to life, and the promise of future accomplishments.

—Gustave Flaubert

What matters most is how well you walk through the fire.

—Charles Bukowski

Chronic pain can be very lonely. It can have a shame-based quality.

—Jennifer Gray

The experience of pain or loss can be a formidably motivating force.

—John C. Maxwell

Don't let pain define you, let it refine you.

—Tim Fargo

Birds sing after a storm; why shouldn't people feel as free to delight in whatever remains to them?

—Rose F. Kennedy

Just because somebody is strong enough to handle pain doesn't mean they deserve it.

—Unknown

In order to rise from its own ashes, a Phoenix first must burn.

—Octavia Butler

Pain nourishes courage. You can't be brave if you've only had wonderful things happen to you.

—Mary Tyler Moore

There is a sacredness in tears. They are not the mark of weakness, but of power. They speak more eloquently than ten thousand tongues. They are messengers of overwhelming grief...and unspeakable love.

— Washington Irving

'Cause everybody hurts
Take comfort in your friends
Everybody hurts
Don't throw your hand
Oh, no
Don't throw your hand
If you feel like you're alone
No, no, no, you're not alone

—R.E.M. – *"Everybody Hurts"*

STRUGGLE: CHARACTER BUILDING IS HARD WORK

Struggle is the food from which change is made, and the best time to make the most of a struggle is when it's right in front of your face.

—Danny Dreyer

Whatever the struggle, continue the climb. It may be only one step to the summit.

—Diane Westlake

The more you've struggled to heal and love yourself, the more in-spiring your story will be to others when you come out the other side full of triumph, awareness, and honour. Don't give up. Your struggle today is the source of your wisdom tomorrow.

—Vironika Tugaleva

Character cannot be developed in ease and quiet. Only through experience of trial and suffering can the soul be strengthened, ambition inspired, and success achieved.

—Nick Vujicic

For the benefit of the roses, we water the thorns too.

—Kari Hohne

In everyday struggle maintain your cool and emotion. To heal a wound you need to stop touching it. Keeping yourself calm in times of stress will not only have immediate smoothing effects; it can also, over time, help you lead a healthier, happier life.

—Dr. Anil Kr Sinha

Out of suffering have emerged the strongest souls; the most mas-sive characters are seared with scars.

—Kahlil Gibran

Craig Hlas

The last 29 days of the month are the toughest!

— Nikola Tesla

STRESS: YOU HAVE IT, BUT DON'T FEED IT

In times of stress, the best thing we can do for each other is to listen with our ears and our hearts and to be assured that our questions are just as important as our answers.

—Fred Rogers

Adopting the right attitude can convert a negative stress into a positive one.

—Hans Selye

Stress is an ignorant state. It believes that everything is an emergency.

—Natalie Goldberg

When we learn to manage that stress, we are able to create our peak performance abilities and remain calm.

—James O'Donnell, *How to Become Patient*

If stress is the villain, humor is the superhero.

—Andrew Tarvin, *Humor That Works*

Doing something that is productive is a great way to alleviate emotional stress. Get your mind doing something that is productive.

—Ziggy Marly

Laughter helps bring balance to a stressful situation.

—Kala Stevenson, *Monday Mornings: A Cup of Laughter*

Playing is for everyone, and it is one of the best ways to relieve stress. Set an hour or two every day to play.

—Rowena Cauba, *Happiness*

The greatest weapon against stress is our ability to choose one thought over another.

— William James

Sometimes when you're overwhelmed by a situation, when you're in the darkest of darkness that's when your priorities are reordered.

— Phoebe Snow

There is more to life than increasing its speed.

— Mohandas K. Gandhi

Stress can actually help you focus better and can be positive. Having small amounts of stress can stimulate you to think. Being able to manage your stress is key.

— Frank Long, *A Better You*

Give your stress wings, and let it fly away.

— Terri Guillemets

PATIENCE: FINDING THE PATIENCE FOR IT

Patience is the art of caring slowly.

—John Ciardi

Patience is the art of hoping.

—Luc de Clapiers

Adopt the pace of nature: her secret is patience.

—Ralph Waldo Emerson

You must first have a lot of patience to learn to have patience.

—Stanislaw J. Lec

Patience is the art of concealing your impatience.

—Guy Kawaski

We must act with clarity, focus, and intent, but we must do so with love, great patience, confidence, and adaptability.

—Akiroq Brost

Patience is the calm acceptance that things can happen in a different order than the one you have in mind.

—David G. Allen

Silence is victory and patience is glory.
Let silence speak our identity
and let patience keep our dignity.

—Aram Seriteratai

Patience is the direct antithesis of anger.
—Allan Lokos, Pocket Peace: *Effective Practices for Enlightened Living*

Patience is not passive; on the contrary, it is concentrated strength.

Silence is victory and patience is glory.

> —Bruce Lee

No one is perfect. We are all a work in progress. Be easy on yourself. Allow yourself some grace. Be patient with yourself.

> —Akiroq Brost

Patience is the master key to every situation. One must have sympathy for everything, surrender to everything, but at the same time remain patient and forbearing.

> —Franz Kafka

Patience can't be acquired overnight. It is just like building a muscle, every day you need to work on it.

> —Eknath Easwaran

Endurance is the crowning quality, and patience all the passion of great hearts.

> —James Russell Lowell

Humility and patience are the surest proofs of the increase of love.

> —John Wesley

Be completely humble and gentle; be patient, bearing with one another in love.

> —Ephesians 4:2

All human power is a compound of time and patience.

> —Honoré de Balzac

Patience makes lighter what sorrow may not heal.

> —Horace

They are ill discoverers that think there is no land, when they see nothing but sea.

> —Francis Bacon

I will not be distracted by noise, chatter, or setbacks. Patience, commitment, grace, and purpose will guide me.

—Louise Hay

Sometimes things aren't clear right away. That's where you need to be patient and persevere and see where things lead.

—Mary Pierce

Life was always a matter of waiting for the right moment to act.

—Paulo Coelho

Patience is also a form of action.

—Auguste Rodin

Patience is the companion of wisdom.

—Saint Augustine

Time heals what reason cannot.

—Seneca

Two things define you: your patience when you have nothing and your attitude when you have everything.

—Unknown

Patience is not a virtue. It is an achievement.

—Vera Nazarian

Patience is the companion of wisdom.

—Unknown

How poor are they that have not patience! What wound did ever heal but by degrees?

—William Shakespeare, *Othello*

Endurance is patience concentrated.

—Thomas Carlyle

RESILIENCE: BEND, DON'T BREAK

Resilient people: are emotionally strong, are kind, gentle and patient, are compassionate even amid personal stress.

> — Amit Sood, *Immerse: A 52-Week Course in Resilient Living*

Our greatest glory is not in never falling, but in rising every time we fall.

> — Confucius

The little reed, bending to the force of the wind, soon stood up again when the storm had passed over.

> — Aretha Franklin

Resilience has a normal rhythm. You may not feel indestructible this morning, but tomorrow you will be strong.

> — Neil Mach, *The Bedevilment of Bertie Lunn*

If you fell down yesterday, stand up today.

> — H.G. Wells

Fall seven times and stand up eight.

> — Japanese proverb

You can be shaped, or you can be broken. There is not much in between.

> — David Foster Wallace

Bend, little willow
Wind's gonna blow you
Hard and cold tonight
Life, as it happens
Nobody warns you
Willow, hold on tight

> — Paul McCartney – *"Little Willow"*

OVERCOMING: GO OVER, AROUND, EVEN THROUGH

It still holds true that man is most uniquely human when he turns obstacles into opportunities.

— Eric Hoffer

When you come out of the storm, you won't be the same person who walked in. That's what this storm's all about.

— Haruki Murakami, *Kafka on the Shore*

Going through things you never thought you'd go through will only take you places you never thought you'd get to.

— Morgan Harper Nichols

Maybe you have to know the darkness before you can appreciate the light.

— Madeleine L'Engle

Ring the bells that still can ring. Forget your perfect offering. There is a crack, a crack in everything. That's how the light gets in.

— Leonard Cohen

One small crack does not mean that you are broken; it means that you were put to the test and you didn't fall apart.

— Linda Poindexter

Although the world is full of suffering, it is also full of overcoming it.

— Helen Keller

A challenge only becomes an obstacle when you bow to it.

— Ray A. Davis

STRENGTH: COMING BACK
FOR ANOTHER ROUND

Strength and growth come only through continuous effort and struggle.

> —Napoleon Hill

Promise yourself to be so strong that nothing can disturb your peace of mind.

> —Christian Larso

In the depth of winter, I finally learned that within me there lay an invincible summer.

> —Albert Camus

Go within every day and find the inner strength so that the world will not blow your candle out.

> —Katherine Dunham

Strength doesn't come from what you can do. It comes from overcoming the things you once thought you couldn't.

> —Rikki Rogers

The real man smiles in trouble, gathers strength from distress, and grows brave by reflection.

> —Thomas Paine

Life is tough, darling, but so are you.

> —Stephanie Bennett-Henry

You never know how strong you are until being strong is the only choice you have.

> —Cayla Mills

You gain strength, courage and confidence by every experience in which you really stop to look fear in the face . . . You must do the thing you think you cannot do.

> —Eleanor Roosevelt

The strongest people are not those who show strength in front of us but those who win battles we know nothing about.

> —Unknown

People cry, not because they're weak. It's because they've been strong for too long.

> —Johnny Depp

It is not the load that breaks you down. It's the way you carry it.

> —Lena Horne

Empaths did not come into this world to be victims, we came to be warriors. Be brave. Stay strong. We need all hands on deck.

> —Anthon St. Maarten

The world breaks everyone, and afterward, some are strong at the broken places.

> —Ernest Hemingway

Never be ashamed about being broken, because strength is nothing but pain that's been repaired.

> —Trent Shelton

Be very strong... be very methodical in your life if you want to be a champion.

> —Alberto Juantoreno

In solitude the mind gains strength and learns to lean upon itself.

> —Laurence Sterne

Strength isn't about how much you can handle before you break. It's about how much you can endure after you've been broken.

> —Unknown

The kind of beauty I want most is the hard-to-get kind that comes from within — strength, courage, dignity.

> —Ruby Dee

It doesn't get easier. You get stronger.

—Unknown

This is my fight song
Take back my life song
Prove I'm alright song
My power's turned on
Starting right now I'll be strong
I'll play my fight song
And I don't really care if nobody else believes
'Cause I've still got a lot of fight left in me
—Rachel Platten – *"Fight Song"*

ENERGY & ENDURANCE: STIR A SENSE OF PURPOSE

Energy and persistence conquer all things.

— Benjamin Franklin

Where attention goes, energy flows; Where intention goes, energy flows.

— James Redfield

There's a direct correlation between positive energy and positive results.

— Joe Rogan

We must change our energy to change our lives.

— Panache Desai

Put your energy into building what is creative, valuable, and empowering. And you won't have to constantly fight against what is destructive and draining.

— Ralph Marston

Concentrate your energy and hoard your strength.

— Sun Tzu

Energy is equal to desire and purpose.

— Sheryl Adams

Energy is contagious: either you affect people or you infect people.

— Unknown

Endurance is one of the most difficult disciplines, but it is to the one who endures that the final victory comes.

— Buddha

It isn't the mountains ahead to climb that wear you out; it's the pebble in your shoe.

— Muhammad Ali

ACTION: WALK ON

The path is made by walking.

— African proverb

The most difficult thing is the decision to act, the rest is merely tenacity.

— Amelia Earhart

Take the first step in faith. You don't have to see the whole staircase, just take the first step.

— Dr. Martin Luther King

Having faith, beliefs, and convictions is a great thing, but your life is measured by the actions you take based upon them.

— Nick Vujicic

Act as if what you do makes a difference. It does.

— William James

Well done is better than well said.

— Benjamin Franklin

You are what you do, not what you say you'll do.

— C.G. Jung

Let's see people. Let's see action. Let's see freedom. Let's see who cares.

— Pete Townshend

It is not how much you do, but how much love you put in the doing.

— Mother Teresa

The soul's joy lies in doing.

— Percy Bysshe Shelley

When you do things from your soul, you feel a river moving in you, a joy.

— Rumi

I am only one, but I am one. I cannot do everything, but I can do something. And I will not let what I cannot do interfere with what I can do.

— Edward Everett Hale

Every morning is bright, beautiful, and gorgeous like the sun, but we can't see it because we are blinded by day-to-day tasks.

— Debasish Mridha

Action may not always bring happiness; but there is no happiness without action.

— Benjamin Disraeli

Light tomorrow with today.

— Elizabeth Barrett Browning

Begin at the beginning and go on until you come to the end; then stop.

— Lewis Carroll

Sentiment without action is the ruin of the soul.

— Edward Abbey

The absent are always wrong.

— French proverb

Don't judge each day by the harvest you reap, but by the seeds you plant.

— Robert Louis Stevenson

I am only one, but I am one. I cannot do everything, but I can do something. And I will not let what I cannot do interfere with what I can do.

— Edward Everett Hale

The humblest tasks get beautified if loving hands do them.

— Louisa May Alcott, Little Women

Concentrate on what you have to do. Fix your eyes on it. Remind yourself that your task is to be a good human being; remind yourself what nature demands of people. Then do it, without hesitation, and speak the truth as you see it. But with kindness. With humility. Without hypocrisy.

— Marcus Aurelius

I get angry about things, and then I go to work.

— Toni Morrison

We must act.

— Marie Curie

And if the darkness is to keep us apart
And if the daylight feels like it's a long way off
And if your glass heart should crack
And for a second you turn back
Oh no, be strong

Walk on, walk on
What you got they can't steal it
No, they can't even feel it
Walk on, walk on
Stay safe tonight

—U2 - "Walk On"

HERO: WHO, ME? YES, YOU.

We do not have to become heroes overnight. Just a step at a time, meeting each thing that comes up ... discovering we have the strength to stare it down.

— Eleanor Roosevelt

We are all ordinary. We are all boring. We are all spectacular. We are all shy. We are all bold. We are all heroes. We are all helpless. It just depends on the day.

— Brad Meltzer

Heroes are made by the paths they choose, not the powers they are graced with.

— Brodi Ashton

When it comes to the pinch, human beings are heroic.

— George Orwell

True heroism is remarkably sober, very undramatic. It is not the urge to surpass all others at whatever cost, but the urge to serve others, at whatever cost.

— Arthur Ashe

Life hits you hard. But it takes you three seconds to decide if you are a superhero or not. I am.

— Hrithik Roshan

Heroes don't have the need to be known as heroes, they just do what heroes do because it is right and it must be done.

— Shannon A. Thompson

What you do makes a difference, and you have to decide what kind of difference you want to make.

— Jane Goodall

I am of certain convinced that the greatest heroes are those who do their duty in the daily grind of domestic affairs whilst the world whirls as a maddening dreidel.

— Florence Nightingale

And then a hero comes along
With the strength to carry on
And you cast your fears aside
And you know you can survive
So when you feel like hope is gone
Look inside you and be strong
And you'll finally see the truth
That a hero lies in you

— Mariah Carey – *"Hero"*

SELF-CARE: YOU CAN'T DO IT WITHOUT YOU

There are days I drop words of comfort on myself like falling leaves and remember that it is enough to be taken care of by myself.

— Brian Andreas

Self-compassion is simply giving the same kindness to ourselves that we would give to others.

— Christopher Germer

Be there for others, but never leave yourself behind.

— Dodinsky

When we truly care for ourselves, it becomes possible to care far more profoundly about other people. The more alert and sensitive we are to our own needs, the more loving and generous we can be toward others.

— Eda LeShan

Rest and self-care are so important. When you take time to replenish your spirit it allows you to serve others from the overflow. You cannot serve from an empty vessel.

— Eleanor Brownn

If your compassion does not include yourself, it is incomplete.

— Jack Kornfield

Put yourself at the top of your to-do list every single day and the rest will fall into place.

— Unknown

By loving yourself more, you love the person you are caring for more.

— Peggi Speers and Tia Walker, *The Inspired Caregiver*

Self-care is never selfish, but it may feel that way when you live a frenzied life.

— Arthur P. Ciaramicoli

Don't let your mind bully your body into believing it must carry the burden of its worries.

— Astrid Alauda

Self-care is how you take your power back.

—Lalah Delia

Self-care is not a waste of time. Self-care makes your use of time more sustainable.

—Jackie Viramontez

Don't forget to pause and nourish yourself a bit along the way. When you're born to help others sometimes you forget to help yourself.

— Paula Heller Garland

Fatigue is the common enemy of us all — so slow down, rest up, replenish, and refill.

—Jeffery R. Holland

If you want to support others you have to stay upright yourself.

— Peter Heg

Your breathing is your greatest friend. Return to it in all your troubles and you will find comfort and guidance.

—Unknown

Our bodies are our gardens to which our wills are gardeners.

— William Shakespeare, *Othello*

No more martyring myself.

— Sharon E. Rainey

That little spark you feel as you heal. That's what life's about.

—Unknown

Craig Hlas

It's not selfish to love yourself, take care of yourself, and to make your happiness a priority. It's necessary.

— Mandy Hale

SELF: SOMEONE WHO DESERVES YOUR LOVE

The most powerful relationship you will ever have is the relationship with yourself.

—Steve Maraboli

You must love yourself before you love another. By accepting yourself and fully being what you are, your simple presence can make others happy.

—Unknown

Drink from the well of yourself and begin again.

—Charles Bukowski

Learning to love yourself is like learning to walk — essential, life-changing, and the only way to stand tall.

—Vironika Tugaleva

If you feel lost, disappointed, hesitant, or weak, return to yourself, to who you are, here and now and when you get there, you will discover yourself, like a lotus flower in full bloom, even in a muddy pond, beautiful and strong.

—Masaru Emoto

You yourself, as much as anybody in the entire universe, deserve your love and affection.

—Sharon Salzberg

Love is the great miracle cure. Loving ourselves works miracles in our lives.

—Louise Hay

CALM: CARRY ON WITH QUIET JOY

When we speak of a calm state of mind or peace of mind, we shouldn't confuse that with an insensitive state of apathy. Having a calm or peaceful state of mind doesn't mean being spaced out or completely empty. Peace of mind or a calm state of mind is rooted in affection, and compassion and is sensitive and responsive to others.

— Dalai Lama XIV

Raise your words, not your voice. It is rain that grows flowers, not thunder.

— Rumi

The wind howls, but the mountain remains still.

— Japanese proverb

There is a calmness to a life lived in gratitude, a quiet joy.

— Ralph H. Blum

You don't have to control your thoughts. You just have to stop letting them control you.

— Dan Millman

Sometimes the most important thing in a whole day is the rest we take between two deep breaths.

— Etty Hillesum

Calmness is the cradle of power.

— Josiah Gilbert Holland

REST: RENEW YOURSELF

You have permission to rest. You are not responsible for everything that is broken. ... For now, take time for you. It's time to replenish.

—Unknown

Everything you do can be done better from a place of relaxation.

—Stephen C. Paul

Your ability to generate power is directly proportional to your ability to relax.

—David Allen

Take rest; a field that has rested gives a bountiful crop.

—Ovid

How beautiful it is to do nothing, and then to rest afterward.

—Spanish proverb

Don't underestimate the value of Doing Nothing, of just going along, listening to all the things you can't hear, and not bothering.

—A.A. Milne, *Winnie the Pooh*

Come to me, all you who are weary and burdened, and I will give you rest.

—Matthew 11:28

Calm mind brings inner strength and self-confidence, so that's very important for good health.

—Dalai Lama

Rest in reason; move in passion.

—Kahlil Gibran

Carry on my wayward son
For there'll be peace when you are done
Lay your weary head to rest

Craig Hlas

Don't you cry no more

— Kansas – "Carry on Wayward Son"

INNER PEACE: A BETTER PLACE

Inner peace is the key: if you have inner peace, the external problems do not affect your deep sense of peace and tranquility. In that state of mind you can deal with situations with calmness and reason, while keeping your inner happiness.

—Dalai Lama XIV

To experience peace does not mean that your life is always blissful. It means that you are capable of tapping into a blissful state of mind amidst the normal chaos of a hectic life.

—Jill Bolte Taylor

Inner peace is priceless as it sprinkles everything you do with joy.

—Roz Fruchtman

Inner peace is impossible without patience. Wisdom requires patience. Spiritual growth implies the mastery of patience. Patience allows the unfolding of destiny to proceed at its own unhurried pace.

—Brian L. Weiss, *Muchas Vidas, Muchos Maestros*

Inner peace can be seen as the ultimate benefit of practicing patience.

—Allan Lokos

Your inner peace is the greatest and most valuable treasure that you can discover.

—Akin Olokun

Set peace of mind as your highest goal, and organize your life around it.

—Brian Tracy

Physical strength is measured by what we carry. Inner strength is measured by what we can bear.

—Unknown

True and lasting inner peace can never be found in external things. It can only be found within. And then, once we find and nurture it with ourselves, it radiates outward.

— Buddha

Learn to calm down the winds of your mind, and you will enjoy great inner peace.

— Remez Sasson

Enjoy the music, art, nature, dreams, thoughtful words, and pleasant images that calm your body, soothe your soul, and restore your inner peace.

— Craig Hlas

Sometimes no words are necessary:

— Lisa Hilton – *"Oasis"*

TRANQUILITY: MAKE STILL THE TEMPEST WITHIN

It is in your power to withdraw yourself whenever you desire. Perfect tranquility within consists in the good ordering of the mind, the realm of your own.

— Marcus Aurelius

Tranquility is a choice. So is anxiety. The entire world around us may be in turmoil. But if we want to be peaceful within. We can.

— Unknown

When you take the time to quiet your mind and not allow anything to intrude on your peace, there is stillness in time. You feel suspended in an ocean of tranquility, and all truth seems to stem from this place of inner understanding.

— John Assaraf

How many times have you noticed it's the little quiet moments in the midst of life that seem to give the rest extra-special meaning?

— Fred Rogers

You can discard most of the junk that clutters your mind — things that exist only there — and clear out space for yourself.

— Marcus Aurelius

When you take the time to quiet your mind and not allow anything to intrude on your peace, there is stillness in time. You feel suspended in an ocean of tranquility, and all truth seems to stem from this place of inner understanding.

— John Assaraf

Within you, there is a stillness and a sanctuary to which you can retreat at any time and be yourself.

— Hermann Hesse

Let us accept the invitation, ever-open, from the stillness, taste its exquisite sweetness, and heed its silent instruction.

—Paul Brunton

Don't try to force anything. Let life be a deep let-go. God opens millions of flowers every day without forcing their buds.

—Osho

The fruit of silence is tranquility.

—Arabian proverb

There are times when we stop, we sit still. We listen and breezes from a whole other world begin to whisper.

—James Carroll

NATURE: DON'T FORGET
THE SOURCE

Those who contemplate the beauty of the earth find reserves of strength that will endure as long as life lasts.

— Rachel Carson, *The Sense of Wonder*

Nature is the best medicine for serenity. Peace, calmness, stillness. It's good for the heart.

— Karen Madwell

One touch of nature makes the whole world kin.

— William Shakespeare, *Troilus and Cressida*

If the sight of the blue skies fills you with joy, if a blade of grass springing up in the fields has the power to move you, if the simple things in nature have a message you understand, rejoice, for your soul is alive.

— Eleonora Duse

Be still, and the world is bound to turn herself inside out to entertain you. Everywhere you look, joyful noise is clanging to drown out quiet desperation.

— Barbara Kingsolver

You will always find an answer in the sound of water.

— Zhuangzi

Heaven is under our feet as well as over our heads.

— Henry David Thoreau

Many eyes go through the meadow, but few see the flowers in it.

— Ralph Waldo Emerson

There is something infinitely healing in the repeated refrains of nature — the assurance that dawn comes after night, and spring after winter.

— Rachel Carson

Let the rain kiss you. Let the rain beat upon your head with silver liquid drops. Let the rain sing you a lullaby.

— Langston Hughes

Never does nature say one thing and wisdom another.

—Junvenal

MUSIC: LET IT HIT YOU

One good thing about music, when it hits you, you feel no pain.
> —Bob Marley

Music is the language of the spirit. It opens the secret of life bringing peace, abolishing strife.
> —Kahlil Gibran

He who sings scares away his woes.
> —Miguel de Cervantes

Music expresses that which cannot be put into words and that which cannot remain silent.
> —Victor Hugo

Life seems to go on without effort when I am filled with music.
> —George Eliot

"Ah, music," he said, wiping his eyes. "A magic beyond all we do here!"
> —J.K. Rowling, *Harry Potter and the Sorcerer's Stone*

Where words fail, music speaks.
> —Hans Christian Andersen

A bird does not sing because it has an answer. It sings because it has a song.
> —Chinese proverb

Music brings a warm glow to my vision, thawing mind and muscle from their endless wintering.
> —Haruki Murakami

Music can change the world.
> —Ludwig van Beethoven

Music can change the world because it can change people.

                                                                — Bono

God knows that I love my music
Ain't no one gonna change my tune
Don't ya know that I love my music
Ain't never gonna change my tune
                    — Loggins and Messina – *"My Music"*

WISDOM: YOU'RE ON THE WAY

Wisdom begins in wonder.

> —Socrates

Logic is the beginning of wisdom, not the end.

> —Leonard Nimoy

Reality + Dreams + Humor = Wisdom.

> —Lin Yutang

All human wisdom is summed up in two words; wait and hope.

> —Alexandre Dumas

The desire to reach for the stars is ambitious. The desire to reach hearts is wise.

> —Maya Angelou

Wisdom is knowing when you can't be wise.

> —Paul Engle

There is a wisdom of the head, and a wisdom of the heart.

> —Charles Dickens

Silence is the sleep that nourishes wisdom.

> —Francis Bacon

The more tranquil a man becomes, the greater is his success, his influence, his power for good. Calmness of mind is one of the beautiful jewels of wisdom.

> —James Allen

Wisdom is nothing more than healed pain.

> —Robert Gary Lee

Even when you have doubts, take that step. Take chances. Mistakes are never a failure — they can be turned into wisdom.

> —Cat Cora

A loving heart is the truest wisdom.

—Charles Dickens

We don't receive wisdom; we must discover it for ourselves after a journey that no one can take for us or spare us.

—Marcel Proust

In wisdom gathered over time I have found that every experience is a form of exploration.

—Ansel Adams

The wisdom acquired with the passage of time is a useless gift unless you share it.

—Esther Williams

Keep me away from the wisdom which does not cry, the philosophy which does not laugh and the greatness which does not bow before children.

—Kahlil Gibran

Let us be silent, content in our little corner, meek and gentle like them. That is the wisdom of life.

—W. Somerset Maugham

He who learns must suffer, and, even in our sleep, pain that cannot forget falls drop by drop upon the heart, and in our own despair, against our will, comes wisdom to us by the awful grace of God.

—Aeschylus

Wisdom is the reward you get for a lifetime of listening when you'd have preferred to talk.

—Doug Larson

Mingle a little folly with your wisdom; a little nonsense now and then is pleasant.

—Horace

INSPIRATION: REKINDLE YOUR MISSION DAILY

May the stars carry your sadness away, may the flowers fill your heart with beauty, may hope forever wipe away your tears, and, above all, may silence make you strong.

— Chief Dan George

Remember, remember, this is now, and now, and now. Live it, feel it, cling to it. I want to become acutely aware of all I've taken for granted.

— Sylvia Plath

You've got to get up every morning with determination if you're going to go to bed with satisfaction.

— George Lorimer

Finish every day and be done with it. You have done what you could; some blunders and absurdities crept in; forget them as soon as you can. Tomorrow is a new day. You shall begin it well and serenely, and with too high a spirit to be cumbered with your old nonsense.

— Ralph Waldo Emerson

Expect problems and eat them for breakfast.

— Alfred A. Montapert

We either make ourselves miserable, or we make ourselves strong. The amount of work is the same.

— Carlos Castaneda

It's good to do uncomfortable things. It's weight training for life.

— Anne LaMott

Start where you are. Use what you have. Do what you can.

— Arthur Ashe

Don't let yesterday use up too much of today.

> —Cherokee proverb

Go as far as you can see; when you get there, you'll be able to see further.

> —Thomas Carlyle

Determination is an inside job, but inspiration comes from the outside.

> —Barbara Aberc

Strength grows in the moments you can't go on, but you keep going anyway.

> —Unknown

In everyone's life, at some time, our inner fire goes out. It is then burst into flame by an encounter with another human being. We should all be thankful for those people who rekindle the inner spirit.

> —Albert Schweitzer

SOME CAREGIVING RESOURCES

There are many terrific **online resources for caregivers**, and these sites will get you started. Several of them link to other national organizations, while others are more self-contained.

National Alliance for Caregiving

Rosalynn Carter Institute for Caregiving

The Caregiver Space

U.S. Dept. of Health and Human Services - Resources for Caregivers

Family Caregiver Alliance - Caregiving at Home: A Guide to Community Resources

SeniorAdvisor.com -- 30 Resources to Help Caregivers

AARP -- Resources Caregivers Should Know About

AARP -- Family Caregiving Basics

CaringBridge - Resources

Care.com - A Guide to Family Caregiver Resources

Caregiver Action Network - Family Caregiver Toolbox

CaregiverStress.com - Caregiver Resources

National Caregivers Library

American Psychological Association - Caregiving Facts

Next Step in Care - Guides and Checklists for Family Caregivers

Johns Hopkins Medicine - Caregiver Resources

Parkinson's Foundation - Caregiver Resources

American Cancer Society - Caregiver Resource Guide

VA Caregiver Support

Happy Healthy Caregiver

Mayo Clinic - Caregiver Stress: Tips for Taking Care of Yourself

Videos

AARP - A Day in the Life of a Caregiver **(2:18)**

TEDx Talks - Caring for the caregivers | Frances Lewis **(14:38)**

TEDx Talks - The joy of now: A caregiver's tale | Phyllis Peters **(10:59)**

Aging and Disability Resources - Caregiver Stress **(4:09)**

CBC News - The National: The Struggle of Being a Caregiver **(2:28)**

University of California Television - Caring for the Caregiver: Fight Caregiver Stress and Prevent Burnout **(57:48)**

Queen Latifah Talks About Caregiving for Her Mom **(2:37)**

Lessons in Caregiving
Evelyn Corsini and her family allowed photographer Francine Orr to document the final months of her life, to observe caregiving.

Images for Inspiration

Michael J. Fox Foundation for Parkinson's Research - For Caregivers

Independence Care System - Caregiver news, tips, stats

899 Best Caregiver Images - Kat

And for some **thoughtful quotes from caregivers themselves**:
The Caregiver Space - 106 Crucial Tips from Fellow Caregivers

Statistics

Statistics on family caregivers and family caregiving:
Caregiver Action Network

5 facts about family caregivers
Pew Research Center

If you've found "Great Quotes For Caregivers" interesting or useful, please consider leaving a short review on Amazon.

Thank you!